Opposites!

HOT AND COLD

BY EMILIE DUFRESNE

BookLife
PUBLISHING

©2018
Book Life
King's Lynn
Norfolk PE30 4LS

ISBN: 978-1-78637-418-9

Printed in Malaysia

Written by:
Emilie Dufresne

Edited by:
Kirsty Holmes

Designed by:
Jasmine Pointer

A catalogue record for this book is available from the British Library.

CONTENTS

Words that look like **this** can be found in the glossary on page 24.

WHAT ARE OPPOSITES?

An opposite is when two things are completely different.

SOME EXAMPLES OF OPPOSITES ARE...

LIGHT AND DARK

HARD AND SOFT

LOUD AND quiet

WET AND DRY

HOT AND COLD

BIG AND small

Something that is **HOT** is not the same as something that is **COLD**.

HOT
AND
COLD
ARE
OPPOSITES.

DESERTS

Deserts are large areas of **barren** land. The Sahara desert in Africa is a very hot desert.

THE SAHARA IS DRY AND HOT.

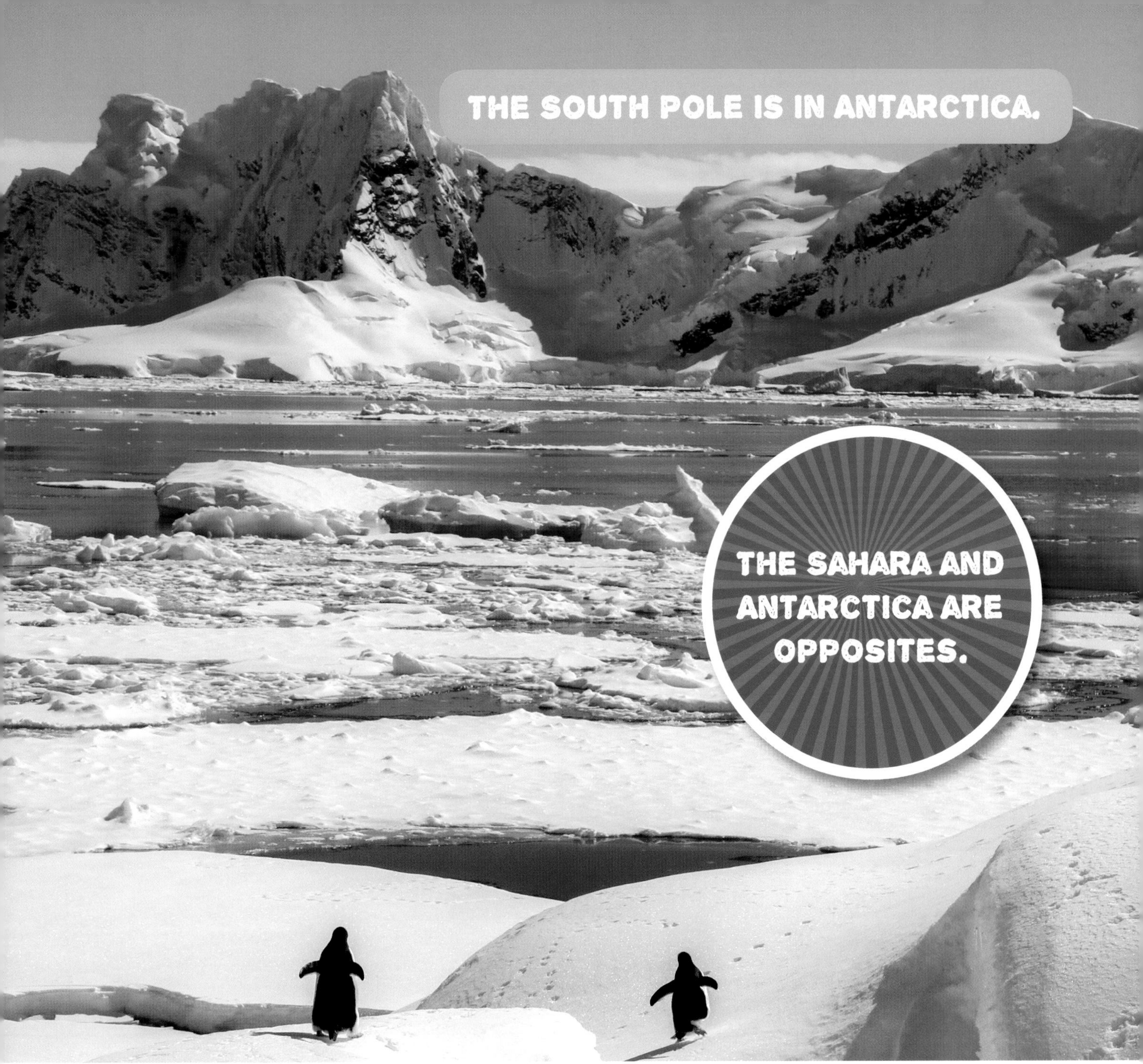

THE SOUTH POLE IS IN ANTARCTICA.
THE SAHARA AND ANTARCTICA ARE OPPOSITES.

Some deserts, like Antarctica, are cold.

FOOD

Some foods are hot. Chillies are spicy and make our mouths feel hot!

CHILLIES AND
ICE CREAM ARE
OPPOSITES!

Some foods, such as ice cream, make your mouth feel cold.

ANIMALS

The sand fox can survive in some of the hottest places on Earth. They live in hot deserts like the Sahara.

THEY HAVE BAT-LIKE EARS TO KEEP THEM COOL.

SAND FOXES AND SIBERIAN TIGERS ARE OPPOSITES.

Siberian tigers live in some of the coldest places on Earth, in temperatures as low as -45 degrees Celsius (°C)!

TEMPERATURE

The hottest temperature ever recorded was in Death Valley, USA. It reached a **sweltering** 56.7 °C.

The coldest temperature ever recorded was in Antarctica. It reached a teeth-chattering -89.2 ºC.

THESE TEMPERATURES ARE OPPOSITES.

HOLIDAYS

Beach holidays are hot holidays. You can play in the sea and make sandcastles.

Skiing holidays are cold holidays. You could go sledding and whoosh down the mountain!

BEACH HOLIDAYS AND SKIING HOLIDAYS ARE OPPOSITES.

DRINKS

Hot chocolate is a hot drink. It keeps you warm in winter.

HOT CHOCOLATES
AND ICED WATER
ARE OPPOSITES!

Iced water is a cold drink. Ice is **frozen** water. It can cool you down on hot days.

PLANETS

Venus is the hottest planet in our **solar system**.
It is the second planet from the Sun.

IT HAS A TEMPERATURE OF AROUND 462 °C!

Neptune is the coldest planet in our solar system.
Its average temperature is around -200 °C.

ACTIVITY

Which of these things are **HOT**, and which are **COLD**?

ICED WATER

BEACH HOLIDAY

ANTARCTICA

HOT CHOCOLATE

SAHARA

SKIING HOLIDAY

ANSWERS

That's right! These ones are **HOT**!

These ones are **COLD**!

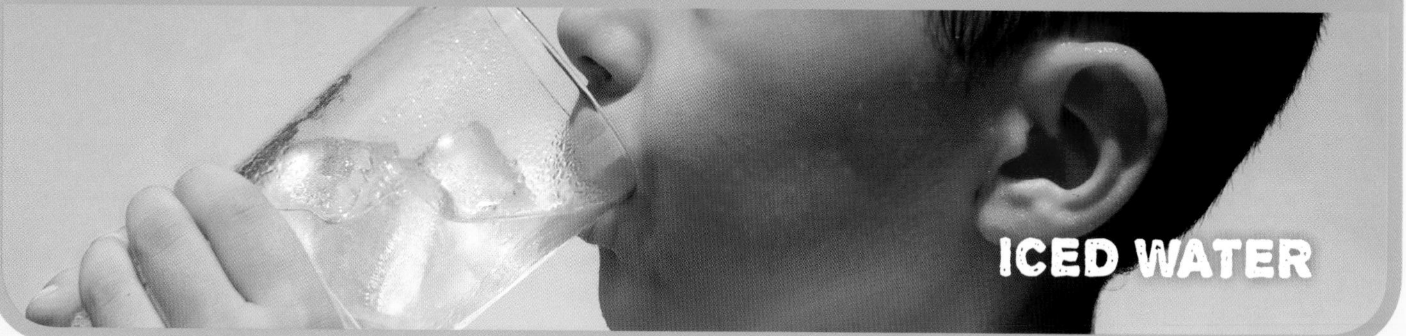

GLOSSARY

barren not able to produce crops

frozen when a liquid becomes a solid in cold temperatures

Siberian of or relating to a place in Northern Asia called Siberia

solar system the system of planets, moons and comets that orbit the Sun

sweltering too hot and too humid

INDEX

Photocredits:
Images are courtesy of Shutterstock.com. With thanks to Getty Images, Thinkstock Photo and iStockphoto.
Front cover - jocic, Tim UR, ANCH, freesoulproduction, Melica, George Dolgikh, rodho, exopixel, Evdeny Karavdaev, TerraceStudio, Valentyn Volkov, Volodymyr Goinyk, barbajones, Africa Studio, Sergey Uryadnikov, gcpics, Virunja. 2 - Frozenmost. 3 – Sergey Uryadnikov, freesoulproduction. 4 – SergiyN. 5 – Budkov Denis, elnavegante. 6 - Yongyut Kumsri. 7 - jeremykingnz. 8 - Jesse Davis. 9 - wavebreakmedia. 10 - Nickolas warner. 11 - Scott E Read. 12 - Sergey Novikov. 13 - river34. 14 - Sunny studio. 15 - gorillaimages. 16 - Sara Winter. 17 - 3445128471. 18 - NASA images. 19 - NASA images. 20 – 3445128471, Sunny studio, jeremykingnz. 21 - Sara Winter, Yongyut Kumsri, gorillaimages. 22 - Yongyut Kumsri, Sunny studio, ara Winter. 23 - jeremykingnz, gorillaimages, 3445128471. 24 - Valentyn Volkov.